VANCOUVER ISLAND
FROM THE AIR

VANCOUVER ISLAND
FROM THE AIR

Photographed by Russ Heinl

Text by Rosemary Neering

Whitecap Books

Vancouver / Toronto / New York

Edited by Elaine Jones
Proofread by Elizabeth McLean
Cover design by Susan Greenshields
Interior design by Margaret Lee

Archival images courtesy of the B.C. Archives and Records Services: p. 12 HP-059655;
p. 17 HP-022847; p. 20 HP-044763; p. 27 A-08282; p. 30 HP-040313; p. 33 HP-072708;
p. 36 I-26675; p. 41 I-21118; p. 44 E-00081; p. 52 I-27586; p. 56 I-27583; p. 60 I-27589;
p. 65 H-04329; p. 68 I-28398; p. 76 I-26128

Printed in Canada.

Canadian Cataloguing in Publication Data

Neering, Rosemary, 1945–
        Vancouver Island from the air

        Includes index.
        ISBN 1-55110-957-3

        1. Vancouver Island (B.C.)—Aerial photographs. I. Heinl, Russ, 1949– II. Title.
FC3844.4.N44 1999   971.1'204'0222   C99-910835-2
F1089.V3N44 1999

The publisher acknowledges the support of the Canada Council for the Arts and the
Cultural Services Branch of the Government of British Columbia for our publishing program.
We acknowledge the financial support of the Government of Canada through the Book
Industry Development Program for our publishing activities.

Dedication

by Russ Heinl

For three wonderful gentlemen, whom I am proud to call my friends, and for whom I have tremendous respect and admiration. Each has taken precious time from his own busy life to encourage and support me in my aerial quests. They have each in their own way achieved international recognition for their varied artistic and creative talents. Had it not been for "a kind word" here and there, I doubt I would have achieved all the aerial goals I set for myself. So a very heartfelt thank you all so very, very much to

Robert Bateman
Ted Grant
Gary McCartie.

Introduction

by Rosemary Neering

The helicopter hovers a few hundred metres from the sheer face of the mountain, the whine of the engine comforting above the Vancouver Island wilderness. Photographer Russ Heinl strains against his safety harness out the open door, bracing himself with his foot on the landing skid. "Take it up," he tells the pilot. "Slide to your nine o'clock. Now back off a little."

As Heinl clicks off frame after frame, the sinking sun turns the peak amber, while the evening light sets blue shadows on serried mountains that fade into the western distance. It is a magic moment. In other times, such a sight was reserved for mountain climbers such as those who have left a record of their achievement in the small cairn on the rock below us. But even mountain climbers cannot achieve quite this perspective, this combination of close-up and all-encompassing that stretches below and beyond us. That view is reserved for those who come, as we have done, by air—and those who see the aerial photographs that result.

The aerial perspective has fascinated photographers since the dawning days of photography. In 1858, the first aerial photographs were taken, capturing the French countryside from the height of a hot-air balloon. But, for all the excitement surrounding those photographs, a balloon provides a limited and static view. Only when airplanes took to the skies did photographers begin to realize the promise of aerial photography. The military were among the first to take advantage of this new perspective, quickly grasping how useful it could be to see enemy territory from above. Cartographers were equally seduced: the ability

7

to photograph from the air made it infinitely easier to map the lines of river and lake and see the contours of mountain and valley.

Scenic photography was less immediately practical, but just as fascinating. Photographers who flew over Vancouver Island from the 1920s on, with mapping or forest inventory as their primary aim, often managed to snap a few scenes of cities and towns, seacoasts and forests, along with their assigned work. By the 1950s, photographers were in the air above Vancouver Island with the sole aim of taking pictures for tourism promotion and publication.

The examples of their black-and-white work in this book, set beside aerials taken today, limn the changes of the island landscape, providing parallel snapshots of then and now. Look down upon central Victoria in 1948, and you see the end of an era, as the last streetcars run on city streets. A 1920s aerial displays ships docked in the Inner Harbour, on their route between Victoria and Vancouver or Seattle, or up the island's west coast. In today's aerials, the streetcars are gone, old buildings have been replaced by new, sailboats tie up where passenger ships used to berth, and motels and office buildings rise where, fifty years ago, open fields and scattered houses lay.

Yet the aerial photographs of then and now also reveal the bones, man-made and natural, that underlie the land-scape. Victoria shows itself as still predominantly a low-rise city, anchored by the Parliament Buildings, the Empress Hotel and the historic stone and brick of Old Town. Ladysmith is instantly recognizable from the air, then and now, and the pattern of the wharves of Ganges on Salt Spring Island is amazingly unchanged. Port Alberni looks much the same now as it did in 1950, Nanaimo is changed and larger but still resting on the same foundations of harbour and city plan, and Sidney—grown well beyond its few blocks of 1950s downtown—is still characterized by its wharves and shoreline.

Those archival photos were taken from fixed-wing aircraft chosen for their ability to fly at slow speed, or for other features that fitted them for aerial photography. However good those aircraft were though, they cannot match today's craft: almost infinitely manoeuvrable, a helicopter can, on command, hover, rise or drop, shimmy back or forward, left or right, and hold position, wind permitting, for as long as the photographer wants. That aerial versatility, combined with modern cameras and films, plus equipment such as gyro stabilizers that eliminate camera shake, means that a photographer can portray a landscape such as Vancouver Island's from an almost infinitely varied perspective, one that can show details that the landbound rarely see or demonstrate the scope of the land, with equal ease.

From the air, Vancouver Island and the Gulf Islands, off the island's east coast in the Strait of Georgia, present a multiplicity of patterns. The Gulf Islands reveal their origins, their glacier-gouged ridges and hollows trending northwest-southeast, their cliffs and pillars sculpted by erosion, their beaches and spits built by the shifting currents.

Fly over Vancouver Island, and you will see a ribbon of settlement, bunched at the southern tip, unrolling along the east coast. Most of the island's 670 000 people live along this ribbon, some 250 kilometres long and just a few kilometres wide, in the coastal communities of Greater Victoria, the Cowichan Valley, Nanaimo, Parksville-Qualicum, the Comox Valley, and Campbell River. The aerial eye in wide view captures the narrowness of this ribbon, then zooms in on turn-of-the-century buildings, a rooftop volleyball court, or a racer piloting a bathtub through coastal waters.

North of Campbell River, this settled strip is interrupted by forests and mountains, to resume with the waterfront communities of the island's northern tip.

From its east coast edge, the Vancouver Island mountains rise. The earthbound eye, looking west, tends to see these mountains as a single spine, but the true pattern is revealed from above, in a series of peaks and valleys that crest, then fall away towards the west coast. Fly that west

coast, and the reason that settlements and roads are concentrated on the east coast becomes apparent. Inlets cut deeply into the jagged coastline, surf foams against the rocks where lighthouses warn of danger, and forests cling to the western slopes of mountains that rise almost from the edge of the sea. The curved sandy beaches hidden between headlands come as a relief to the eye, just as the few calm inlets came as a relief to early mariners who sought landfall along this coast.

Near one of these headlands, the helicopter hovers so low that the downdraft from its blades sends ripples skidding across the water. Russ Heinl once more directs the pilot, up, down, left, right, seeking the best vantage point over the frothing surf, the cleft rocks, and the caves and arches that border the thin crescent of beach below. This perspective, so different from that available from land or water, makes the island shores almost as new to today's viewer as they were to those mariners of two centuries ago. Following and greatly expanding on the tradition begun by the photographers who took the first black-and-white aerials of Vancouver Island, Heinl's often amazing views from the air give us new insight into our island landscapes.

Victoria's downtown surrounds the harbour, anchored by the Parliament Buildings, centre. The Royal British Columbia Museum is at left, with the former Canadian Pacific Navigation Company steamship terminal built in 1924 and now housing the Wax Museum in the foreground on the water.

Then and Now

In the 1920s, when this archival photograph was taken, a variety of coastal ships took on and dropped off passengers at docks in Victoria's harbour. The Triangle Run served Victoria, Seattle and Vancouver; coastal service ran between Victoria, Bamfield, Port Alberni, Port Alice, and points in between. Today's Inner Harbour is just as busy, but with more floatplanes and pleasure craft than ferries or ships. The Victoria–Port Angeles ferry and catamarans that travel to Seattle are the only large ships that dock in the harbour today.

ABOVE The Grand Old Lady of Victoria's hotels, The Empress, looks out over the Inner Harbour. A Canadian Pacific Railway hotel, it was built in 1908, added to in 1929, refurbished in the 1960s and again added to in 1989.

RIGHT A gilded Captain George Vancouver, the British explorer who charted much of British Columbia's coastal waters in the late eighteenth century, stands atop the copper-roofed dome of the Parliament Buildings.

The Parliament Buildings and the lawn in front of them have changed little
in the fifty years between this 1947 archival photograph and the present day.
But the tennis courts next to the buildings, used by government employees,
are long gone, and the neighbourhood near the buildings is now crowded
with motels, hotels and apartment buildings.

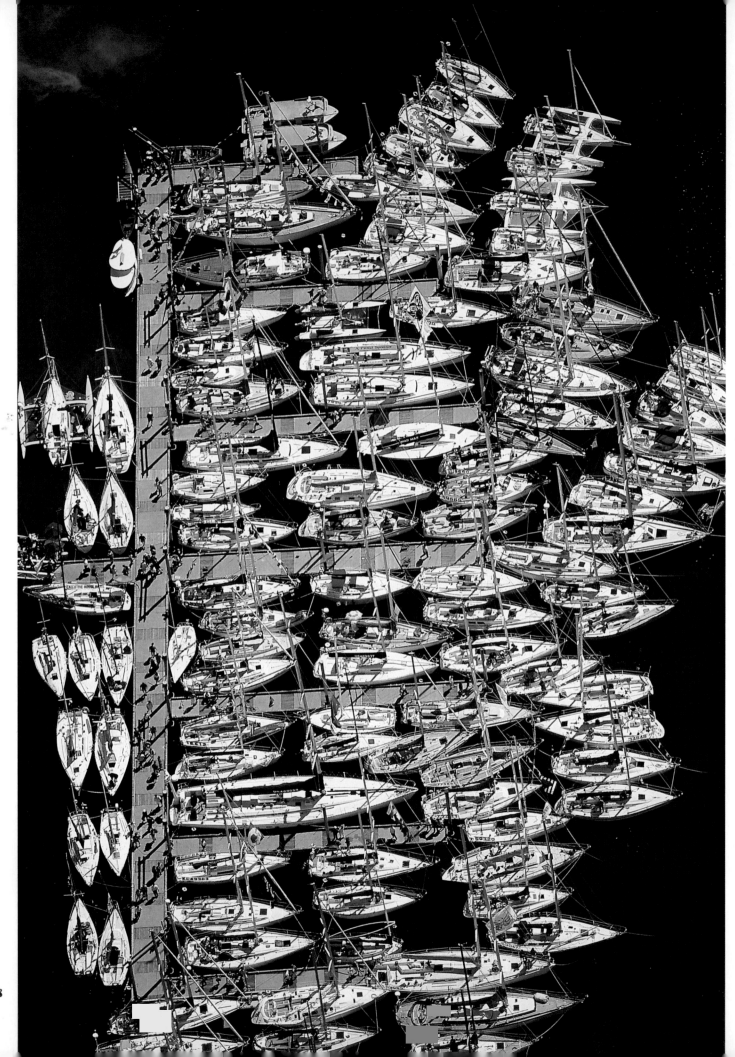

RIGHT A boat under sail in one of the Swiftsure races: the main 138-mile Swiftsure Bank course, the 100-mile Cape Flattery race, and the 76-mile Juan de Fuca course. The events take place the last weekend in May.

LEFT Boats cluster in the Inner Harbour the day before the start of Swiftsure, the sailing race that has brought boaters to Victoria since 1930. Swiftsure attracts several hundred boats and big crowds of spectators every year.

Then and Now

In April 1957, Government House, the residence of British Columbia's lieutenant-governor, burned down; its smouldering remains are shown in this archival photograph the morning after the fire. The present Government House is the third on the site. The first, Cary Castle, was built in 1860 for British Columbia's attorney general, and sold to the government in 1865. That damp, drafty building was not much mourned when it burned down in 1899. The second vice-regal residence, designed by noted architects Samuel Maclure and Francis Rattenbury in a rare and uneasy collaboration, replaced the first in 1903 and served until the 1957 fire. The current building was designed along the traditional lines of the mansion it replaced.

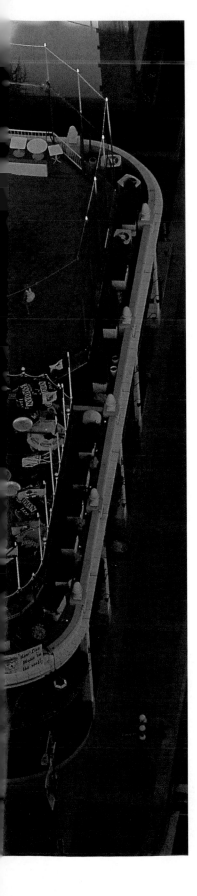

LEFT Onlookers sip drinks as players take to the sand-covered court at the Rooftop Volleyball Court Lounge, part of the Strathcona Hotel in downtown Victoria.

ABOVE Robert Dunsmuir built Craigdarroch Castle for his wife, Joan, in the 1890s, but he died before the couple could move in. Joan lived there until her death; since then, the castle has served as quarters for a private hospital and Victoria College in its early years. Restored to its turn-of-the-century grandeur, it is now a major tourist attraction.

The lights on the Parliament Buildings were first illuminated in 1897, in honour of Queen Victoria's diamond jubilee, the year before the buildings officially opened. They remain the focus of downtown Victoria by night.

This archival photograph taken in 1948, looking north from Yates along Douglas Street, truly shows the end of the line: that was the year the last streetcar ran on Victoria streets. The British Columbia Electric Rail System once operated as far north as Sidney; its city lines in Victoria carried passengers to the waterfront, through Oak Bay and along the Gorge Waterway. But motor buses replaced the last streetcar in 1948, and the tracks shown in this photograph were torn up. Some buildings differ in the archival and modern aerial views of these streets, but Victoria's low-key streetscape is still recognizable.

ABOVE Strollers wander the waterfront of the Inner Harbour, past a building that was originally a gas station, with storage and car repair underneath. It now houses Victoria's tourist information office and a restaurant.

RIGHT What is now Victoria's Market Square, at the north end of downtown, contained hotels, bars and brothels, the lure for many a sailor who came ashore from the city's bustling late-nineteenth-century harbour. The buildings on Johnson, Store and Pandora streets were restored in the 1970s, and now attract people to shopping, dining and shows in the centre courtyard.

Then and Now

This aerial view from behind the Parliament Buildings and Empress Hotel, looking across Victoria's Inner Harbour towards Esquimalt, was taken in 1934. The Songhees land, centre, had been acquired from the Songhees Indian Band in 1910, and was being used for industry. The blue bridge—the Johnson Street Bridge which links downtown Victoria and Victoria West—was ten years old, and the entrance to the Gorge Waterway was edged with wharves. The Blue Bridge, a lift span, still opens to allow larger boats access to the Gorge, but the Songhees lands are mightily changed: faux-chateau condominium buildings built in the late 1980s and the 1990s now occupy much of the land, and a walkway leads along the waterfront.

Then and Now

By the time this photograph was taken in about 1953, Naden, the barracks and training area of Canadian Forces Base Esquimalt, was somewhat quieter than during World War II, when Esquimalt was the headquarters for the Canadian Navy's Pacific Command. But there was still considerable activity: the Nelles Building, top centre, had just opened, and ships such as the *Stone Town*, lower left, a navy ship converted to weather-ship duty, sailed from home base here. The Nelles Building still anchors the modern photograph, but the white anti-aircraft tower present in 1953 has been torn down, a parade square replaces the scatter of buildings at the photo's centre, and pleasure boats now tie up at the wharf.

Every year, the twenty hectares of The Butchart Gardens
attract nearly one million people from around the world,
who come to marvel at the spring bulbs, the summer
bedding plants and roses, and the twinkling lights that
illuminate the gardens in winter. The Sunken Garden
shown here was one of the first gardens created at
Butchart, in 1908.

Then and Now

One of a series of aerials taken of Vancouver Island in 1957, this photograph shows the wharf at the end of Beacon Avenue—Sidney's main street—the town's shoreline, a few blocks of houses backed by farm fields, and the lone runway of Victoria Airport in the background. Much has changed in the modern photo: the Beacon Avenue wharf remains, though much truncated, a boat basin and series of shops and restaurants fills in the harbour area, and houses, malls, hotels and stores have mushroomed west towards the airport. The Patricia Bay Highway, barely visible in the archival photograph, was opened through to Swartz Bay in 1960, a year after the airport was upgraded to Victoria International Airport. And Sidney's population multiplied some tenfold, from just over 1000 in the early 1950s to 11 000 now.

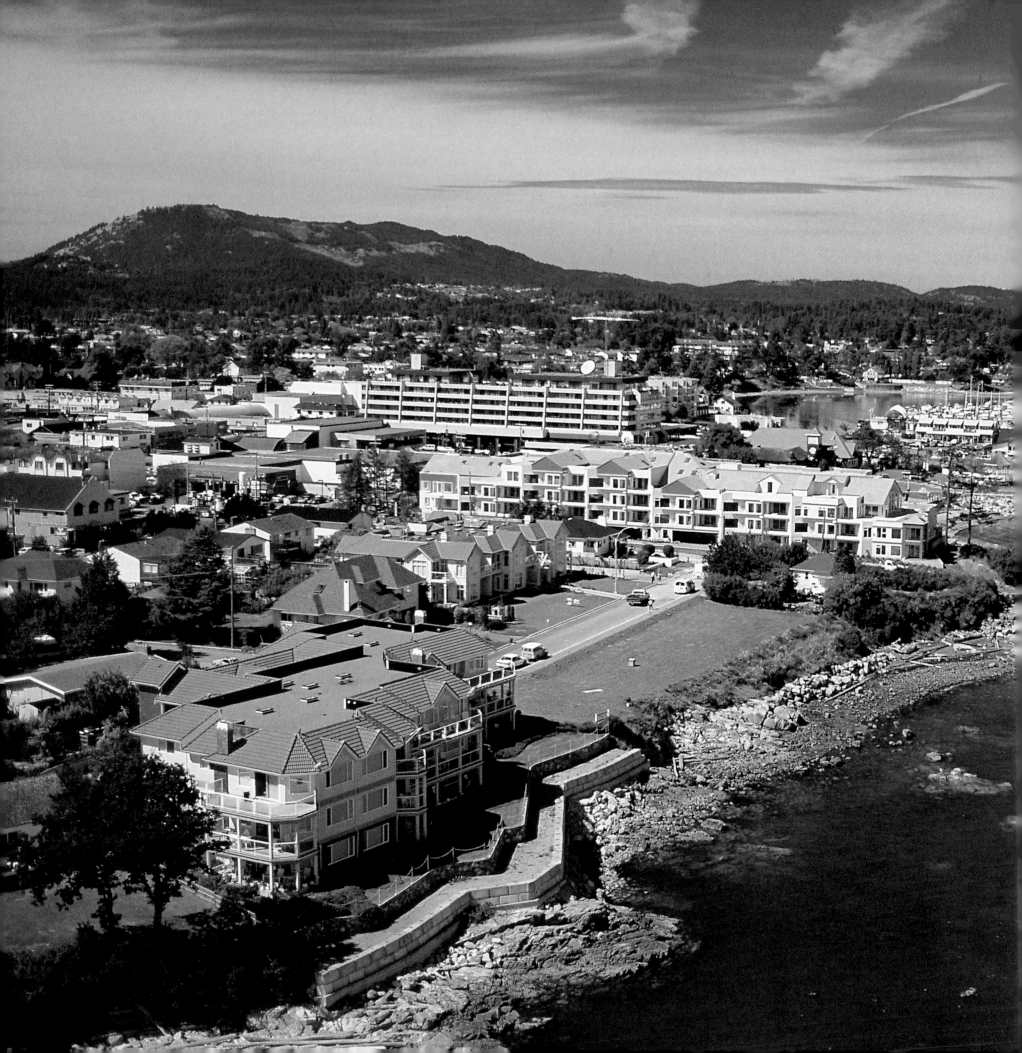

New condominiums and walkways border the waterfront of Sidney, north of Victoria on the Saanich Peninsula. Major construction over the last decade has transformed the town's seashore.

Three-hundred-hectare James Island was a busy place in 1957, when this aerial photograph was taken. Offshore about five kilometres southeast of Sidney, James Island was bought by Canadian Explosives Ltd. in 1913. The company set up a manufacturing plant for TNT, in great demand during World War I, and supported it with a small community of houses and a school, wharves, and two small railway lines. Manufacturing was cut back considerably in 1962, and the settlement abandoned; the plant closed for good in 1978. Today's aerial shows a much more pastoral scene. Only a few people still live on James Island.

LEFT Sidney Island, in Haro Strait near the international border, provides long sandy beaches and a haven for boaters in its protected harbour off Sidney Spit. A foot-passenger ferry from Sidney provides access to the campsites, lagoon, meadows and forest of the island, which is a provincial marine park.

RIGHT Salt Spring's Ganges Harbour cuts a deep U-shape into the island. The town of Ganges, at the end of the harbour, is the largest in the Gulf Islands, with a population of 800.

Then and Now

There has been a Mouats' store in Ganges, on Salt Spring Island, since 1907, when Jane Mouat bought out an existing store. Since then, the Mouat family has run the business at this same location, centre right in both this 1930 archival and the modern photograph. The pattern of wharves that lead out beside the store remains the same as well, but much else has changed: the point is now occupied by recently built condominiums, and the nearby parking lots and streets are clogged with cars.

At its easternmost tip, Saturna, the most remote of the southern Gulf Islands served by BC Ferries, curves in a crescent into the Strait of Georgia.

LEFT A private yacht motors through Active Pass, between Mayne and Galiano islands. The pass is a busy marine highway: ferries that travel between Vancouver Island and the mainland sail through here, as do many pleasure boats. It also welcomes marine life. Cormorants, loons, gulls, bald eagles, sea lions, porpoises and killer whales frequent the area.

RIGHT The aerial vantage point is ideal for showing the effects of long-ago glacial action that scoured the channels between the Gulf Islands and sharpened the ridges that characterize many of the islands. Shown here is Prevost Island, near Salt Spring.

Ferries pass each other in the narrow confines of Active
Pass—5.5 kilometres long, 550 to 1700 metres wide,
with two right-angle turns. The pass links the Strait of
Georgia to the channels and sounds that divide the Gulf
Islands and lead to southern Vancouver Island.

Then and Now

1955 was an exciting year for Crofton: Western Forest Industries announced they would build a pulp mill in this town at the edge of Osborne Bay northeast of Duncan. An instant town created to serve the smelter that was built in 1902 for ore from nearby Mount Sicker and other areas, Crofton boomed for a brief decade, then dwindled when the smelter closed. The pulp mill, shown here under construction in 1957, revived Crofton, which also got a ferry link to Salt Spring Island in the mid-1950s. The familiar plume of mill smoke still rises over the town today.

The Cowichan River foams between rocky shores near Duncan on southern Vancouver Island. The river winds 47 kilometres from Cowichan Lake through a broad valley to tidewater in Cowichan Tribes land at Cowichan Bay.

Then and Now

Chemainus has been linked with logging and lumber-milling since the 1860s, so it's familiar with the boom-and-bust cycle of the forest industry. Its mill burned down in 1923, but a new, larger mill was built on the same site. Log booms and lumber piles in this photograph, taken in 1957, testify to the town's prosperity. But the mill closed in the 1980s, and Chemainus took on new life as a tourist town, known for the many murals painted on the sides of its buildings. Now, a new mill has reopened, though on a smaller scale than in earlier times.

A BC Ferries dock and landing leads towards the fields and forests of Thetis Island, northeast of Chemainus. The small island, population 235, attracts cyclists to its quiet roads and canoeists and kayakers to its shores.

Then and Now

The neat blocks of Ladysmith front on the Island Highway, which separates the residential part of town from the industrial waterfront in this 1957 photograph. Ladysmith was founded to provide housing for coal miners working nearby mines south of Nanaimo. It was named for the South African town of the same name after a decisive battle in the Boer War. Ladysmith still gives the same neat impression from the air, though waterfront homes have replaced some of the industrial activity, and pleasure boats now tie up where log booms were corralled.

Pacific white-sided dolphins leap and play in ocean waters. These mammals are community-minded: they travel in groups that can contain as many as a thousand animals.

The building of the Harmac pulp mill in Cedar, south of Nanaimo, was part of the forest industry boom in the late 1940s and 1950s. Construction began on the H.R. MacMillan Export Company mill in 1948. The first run of unbleached pulp took place in 1950, the same year that this photograph was taken. The mill doubled in size in 1950; with 500 employees, it was a mainstay of the Nanaimo economy. The modern aerial shows today's mill, one of Canada's largest pulp producers, turning out five different grades of pulp for uses that range from telephone directories to medical gowns. Harmac employs about 600 people.

The eroded sandstone shelves of Gabriola Island, near
Nanaimo, give the island's shores a look all their own.
Gabriola's sandstone has been quarried for building and
for pulpstones used to grind raw logs into pulp. It also
forms waterfront galleries where waves have sculpted
the stone into overhanging curves.

Then and Now

Nanaimo's characteristic pinwheel streets are no longer as evident in modern photographs as they were in this 1957 archival aerial: in the last four decades the town has spread beyond its base on the harbour and the hill into the Harewood Valley and almost to the slopes of Mount Benson beyond. Part of the inlet has been filled in for parking lots, and major condominium construction along the water parallels the pleasure and fishing boat harbour.

LEFT Mount Arrowsmith rises to 1817 metres in the Vancouver Island Mountains between Parksville and Port Alberni. The regional park on the mountain features downhill and cross-country skiing, rock and ice climbing, and hiking.

ABOVE Since the first contestants motored the often chaotic course between Nanaimo and Vancouver in 1967, Nanaimo's International World Championship Bathtub Race in July has evolved to a safer affair over a 58-kilometre triangular course that begin Nanaimo's harbour and ends at Departure Bay. Bathtubbers must still adhere to strict rules: among them, tubs must conform to the shape and design of an old-style roll-rim bathtub and be powered by no more than an eight-horsepower motor.

The departing tide reveals a pattern of whorls and ridges
in the shallow intertidal zone along Parksville's seashore.
Every summer, vacationing families enjoy the long,
gently sloping beaches and the warm water in this
east coast area of the island.

Parksville's main street, restored to a gentler pace now
that fast traffic bypasses town on the Island Highway,
cuts a lighted line through the town at sunset.

Then and Now

Plumes of smoke still rise above the pulp mill at Port Alberni, though activity is reduced from the glory days in the mid-1950s, when the mill was being expanded. Then the city was in transition: the last passenger train left Port Alberni in 1957, logging by rail was being replaced by truck logging, the road to Tofino on the west coast would open in 1959, and the twin cities of Port Alberni and Alberni were about to be amalgamated. From the air, today's city looks much like it did four decades ago, though tourism helps support it now that logging and milling are shrinking.

RIGHT A windsurfer flies across the waves. Favourite locations for wind-surfers are Victoria's waterfront off Dallas Road, where surfers take advantage of strong winds that blow in off Juan de Fuca Strait, and Nitinat Lake, a tidal inlet on the island's southwest coast.

LEFT Inlets and channels lead from Clayoquot Sound deep into the forested hills that border Vancouver Island's west coast. Clayoquot is a name known round the world for the battles waged on the shores of the sound to protect its old-growth temperate rain forests from logging.

At the entrance to the open Pacific north of Pacific Rim National Park, 65-kilometre-long Clayoquot Sound is edged by white sand beaches and dotted with tiny islands. The sound and its shores support a wealth of plant and animal species.

Steller sea lions poke inquisitive snouts towards the helicopter from their rocky perches. The mammals are known for their raucous barks, their not-always-welcome smell, and their smooth underwater skills.

The town of Tofino lies facing Clayoquot Sound at the end of the Esowista Peninsula north of Pacific Rim National Park. Since the park was established and the road from the island's east coast greatly improved, Tofino has been transformed from a town supported mainly by logging and fishing to a tourism-services town.

There's been a Wickaninnish Inn on the west coast
for many decades. This luxury resort overlooking the
long curve of Chesterman Beach south of Tofino has a
growing reputation for its food. It is the second to bear
the name Wickaninnish: the first was converted into a
restaurant and ocean-interpretation centre for Pacific
Rim National Park.

RIGHT Surfers, protected from the chilly Pacific waters by wetsuits, walk along the edge of Long Beach, a favourite destination for the surfing and surf-kayaking crowd.

LEFT The classic curve of Long Beach—one of the quintessential west coast images—attracts thousands every year for swimming, sunning and winter storm-watching. The beach is the centrepiece of Pacific Rim National Park, more than 50 000 hectares of sand beaches, rocky shorelines and west coast rain forest.

LEFT Waves have hollowed out caves and arches along the island's west coast north of Clayoquot Sound.

RIGHT Waves break offshore from Pacific Rim National Park, on Vancouver Island's west coast. Designation of the area as a national park preserved broad tracts of forest, where hemlock, Sitka spruce and cedar grow almost to the water's edge.

RIGHT The Cape Beale lighthouse has marked the rock-guarded entrance to Barkley Sound on Vancouver Island's west coast since 1873. Its lighthouse keepers have seen many a gale and shipwreck, and rescued many mariners in trouble.

LEFT Ucluelet's protected harbour and wharves provide shelter in Ucluelet Inlet for pleasure craft and commercial fish boats. The town, at the southern end of the Pacific Rim highway, makes its living from fishing, logging and tourism. Its name derives from the Nuu-chah-nulth word for "wind blowing into the bay."

These eroded cliffs, forest, and rough and daunting
waves are among the features along the West Coast Trail.
Built as a lifesaving and communications trail because of
shipwrecks in this, the graveyard of the North Pacific,
the trail is now so popular that limits must be imposed
on the number of hikers who brave its 77 kilometres.

LEFT Robert Van Sprang, lighthouse keeper at Pachena Point lighthouse on the West Coast Trail, gets a close-up view of the photographer's helicopter.

ABOVE A grey whale surfaces, one of more than 20 000 that migrate through the waters off the west coast of Vancouver Island each spring and fall. Their 10 000-kilometre trek between the waters off Baja California and the Bering Sea is the longest migration undertaken by mammals anywhere on earth.

The action of the waves shapes bars and beaches such as these at Sandy Island Marine Park. At very low tide, a sandbar connects the park to Denman Island, reached by ferry from south of Courtenay.

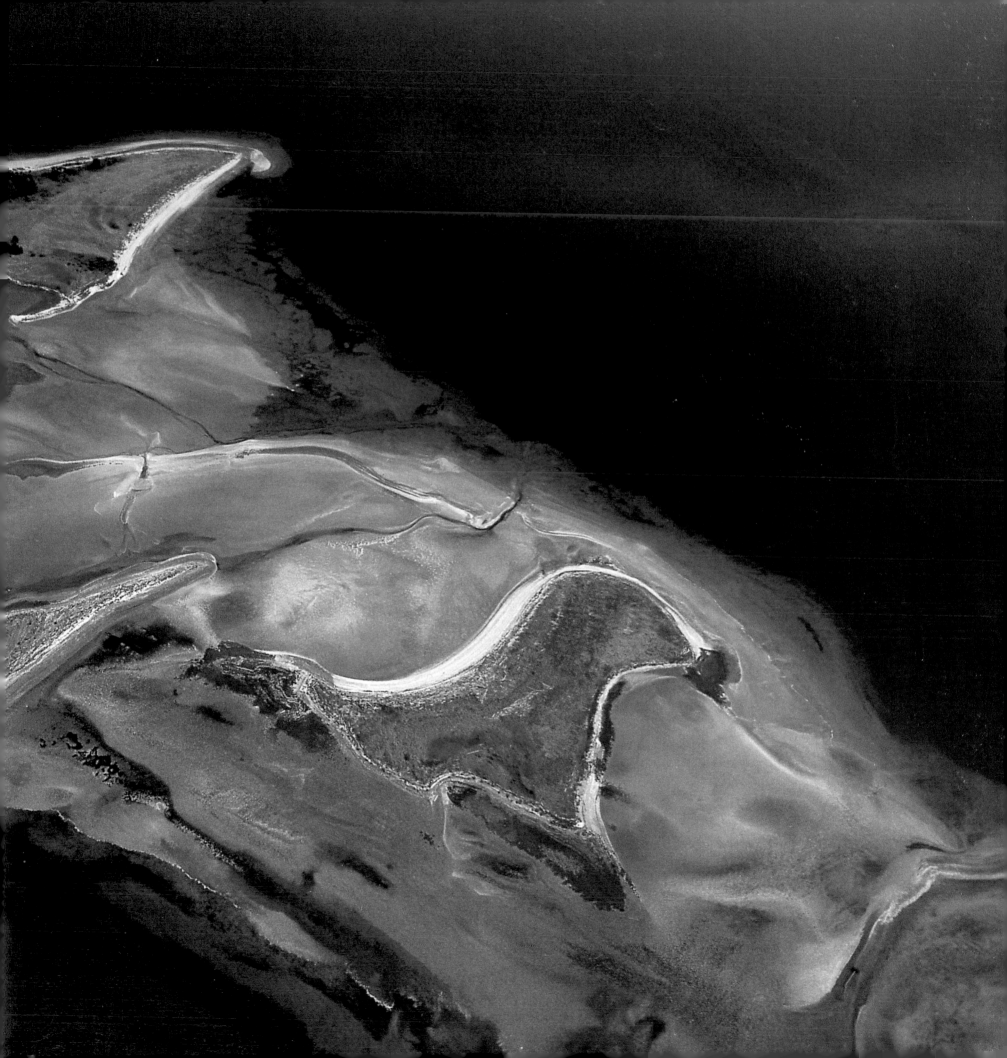

Sailboats anchor off the sandy beaches and shallow waters of Hornby Island, a two-ferry trip from Vancouver Island via Denman Island. Thousands of vacationers swell the population of 30-square-kilometre Hornby each summer, drawn by these beaches, dramatic cliffs and caves, and the laid-back lifestyle.

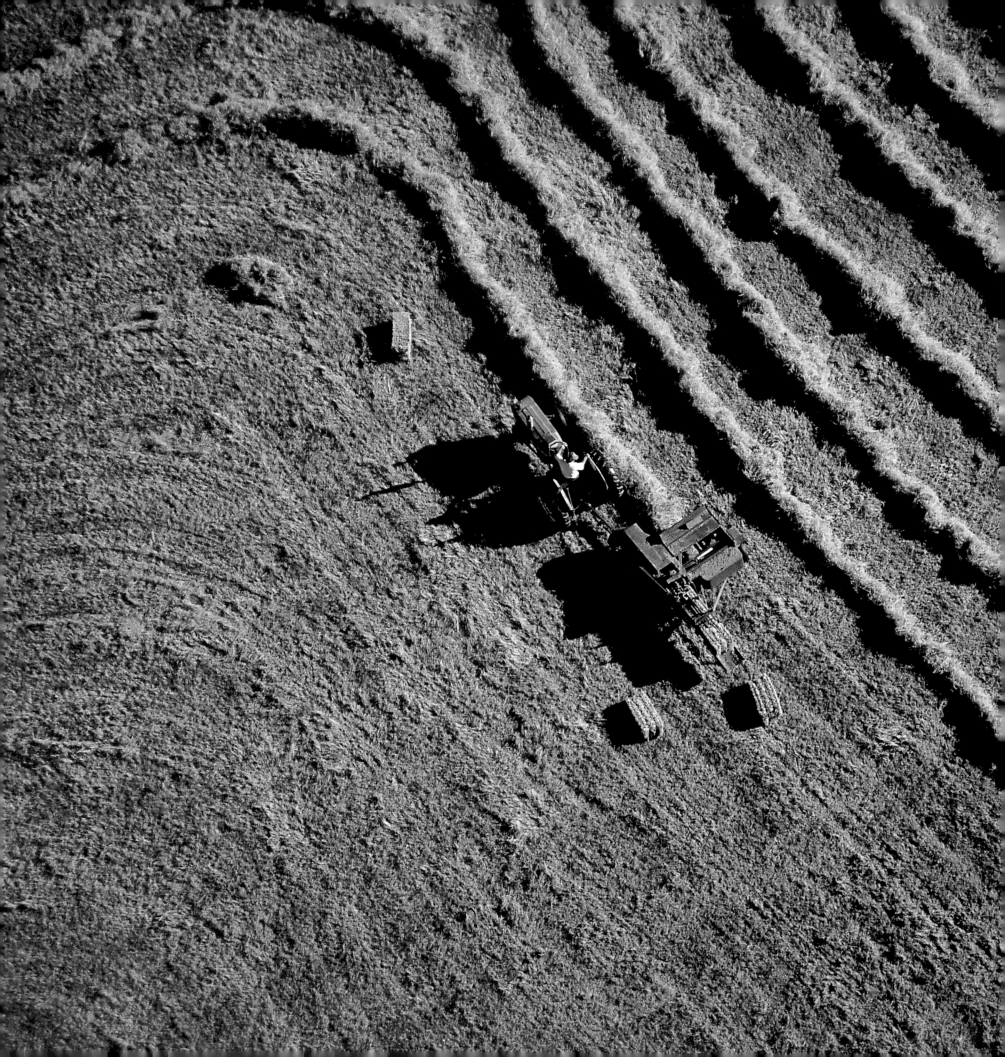

A farmer bales hay on Hornby Island, where small farms and vegetable patches occupy cleared and fertile corners. Well known for the craftspeople who live here, Hornby has long been a treasured retreat for those who call it home.

Mount Washington, shown here from the west with the Strait of Georgia glimmering blue in the distance, is the island's premier ski hill, with five ski lifts and more than twenty downhill runs, plus groomed cross-country trails.

ABOVE The Canadian Forces air demonstration squadron, the Snowbirds, complete a loop in tight formation offshore from the Canadian Armed Forces Comox Air Base. The team of 21 pilots and technical crew fly their nine CT-114 Tutor jets at some 70 air shows every year.

RIGHT Della Falls, at 440 metres the highest waterfall in Canada, cascades down the rocks near the southern boundary of Strathcona Provincial Park.

RIGHT Yuquot—dubbed Friendly Cove by a trader in 1786—is a long-time Nuu-chah-nulth settlement. In the late eighteenth century, it was the centre of European civilization on the west coast and site of the signing of the historic Nootka Convention between British and Spanish interests. On Nootka Island in Nootka Sound, Yuquot is a seasonal gathering place for area Nuu-chah-nulth.

LEFT Snow frosts the shady side of Red Pillar Rock year-round. The peak, named for its shape and deep red colour, is near the southern border of Strathcona Provincial Park on central Vancouver Island.

Sunshine glints through Pacific clouds, turning Quatsino Sound, on northwestern Vancouver Island, silver and moody. The sound and its attached inlets cut across the island from the west coast almost to the east coast.

RIGHT One of the few parts of British Columbia not overridden by glaciation, the spade-shaped Brooks Peninsula on the west coast of northern Vancouver Island is valued for its unique flora. Offshore lives B.C.'s only population of sea otters, reintroduced here decades after they were extirpated by hunters.

LEFT The waves roll in across the unbroken Pacific, near Cape Scott on the island's northwest tip. Danish settlers who tried to colonize this region at the turn of the century were defeated by its ruggedness and isolation. Trails and the occasional overgrown clearing in the bush are the only reminders of their presence in what is now Cape Scott Provincial Park.

Port Hardy, the northernmost town on Vancouver Island, is the southern terminus for ferry routes to Prince Rupert and Bella Coola. Almost 500 kilometres north of Victoria and the island's southern tip, Port Hardy is sustained by fishing, the forest industry and tourism.

The sun sets over the Strait of Georgia and Vancouver Island, in the far distance. Freighters standing off Vancouver's harbour are in the foreground.

72

Index

Acknowledgements

Long Beach Helicopters is pleased to sponsor this book since it shows the views that we, as pilots, experience daily and at times may take for granted.

Long Beach Helicopters started operating in 1976 from a base at the Tofino Airport on the west coast of British Columbia. In 1980, the company opened a second base in Nanaimo and most recently a third one in Campbell River. We operate Eurocopter AS 350Bs exclusively because they are reliable, comfortable and safe.

Our helicopters have operated in almost every province in Canada and we have been involved in fire fighting, surveys, forestry, mining, communications, tourism, medical evacuations, aerial photography, motion picture photography, and more. In the last few years, we have provided specialty tours such as heli-fishing, wildlife viewing, and flights over the Inside Passage and wilderness areas not accessible by other means.

Long Beach Helicopters would like to thank various government agencies, mainly NAV Canada for its support in directing traffic and providing aircraft separations on photo shoots around Victoria and Vancouver.

Long Beach Helicopters can be reached at 2363 Cienar Drive, Nanaimo, BC V9T 3L6. Telephone: (250) 758-0024. Fax: (250) 758-2531.